The life cycle of a
Frog

Ruth Thomson

WAYLAND

First published in 2006 by Wayland
an imprint of Hachette Children's Books

British Library Cataloguing in Publication Data
Thomson, Ruth
  The life cycle of a frog. - (Learning about life cycles)
  I. Frogs - Life cycles - Juvenile literature
  I Title
  571.8'1789

Editor: Victoria Brooker
Designer: Simon Morse
Senior Design Manager: Rosamund Saunders

Printed and bound in China

Hachette Children's Books
A division of Hodder Headline Limited
338 Euston Road, London NW1 3BH

Photographs: pages 2, 6 Kim Taylor/naturepl.com;
cover main image, 4-5 David Kjaer/naturepl.com;
cover inset pictures, 7, 11, 12, 13, 14, 15, 16, 17, 18,
19, 23 Jane Burton, naturepl.com; 8 Michael
Maconachie; Papilio/CORBIS; 9, 23 John
Cancalosi/naturepl.com; 10 and 23 Philippe
Clement/naturepl.com; 20 Andrew
Cooper/naturepl.com; 21 Photofusion Picture
Library / Alamy; p22 George
McCarthy/naturepl.com

ISBN-13: 978-0-7502-4859-4
ISBN-10: 0-7502-4859-9

Contents

Frogs live here

Common frogs live in dark, damp places near water. They spend most of their time on land, where they can find food.

What is a frog?

A frog is an amphibian, an animal that can live on land and in water. It can crawl, swim and dive. It jumps a long way with its strong back legs.

large, sharp eyes
for spotting **prey**

smooth, damp skin

long toes

big **webbed feet** to
push though water

long back legs

Time to lay eggs

Every spring, frogs make their way to the pond where they were born. Each male sits in the water and **croaks** noisily to a female.

The male sits on top of the female
and holds her very tightly.
The female lays her eggs in the water
and the male **fertilises** them.

Frogspawn

The eggs are called frogspawn.
Each egg is surrounded by a ball
of clear jelly. They stick together
in a clump.

Each black egg slowly changes
shape, growing longer and
bigger. After a week, it is
a tiny tadpole with
a head and a tail.

Hatching

When the tadpoles are ready to **hatch**, they push their way out of the jelly. At first, they are weak and cling onto pondweed.

The young tadpoles grow feathery **gills** for breathing. The gills take in **oxygen** from the water. The tadpoles start eating **algae**.

2 weeks

4 weeks

Tadpoles

The small tadpoles swim together in **shallow** water. They nibble plants and grow longer. Their feathery **gills** disappear. Now they breathe with gills inside their body.

The tadpoles become meat-eaters.
They catch water fleas and flies.
They nibble dead fish.

Growing legs

Two bumps appear on the tadpole's body, either side of its tail. The bumps grow into back legs with **webbed feet**.

7 weeks

Soon front legs grow. **Lungs** grow inside the tadpole's body. It swims to the surface to breathe in air.

9 weeks

Froglet

Every day, the tadpole looks more and more like a frog. Its tail shortens. It starts swimming with its **webbed** back feet.

12 weeks

15 weeks

Now, the tiny froglet has no tail at all. It hops out of the pond. It hides near the water's edge. Birds, fish and snakes often eat froglets.

Adult frog

The frog lives in a damp spot
all summer and autumn.
It eats insects, worms,
spiders and slugs.
It grows much bigger.

6 months

When cold winter comes,
the frog cannot keep warm.
It goes into a deep sleep
at the bottom of a ditch or pond.
This is called hibernation.

2 years

Ready to mate

In spring, when the weather warms up, the frog wakes up. It returns to the pond to find a **mate** and lay new frogspawn.

Frog life cycle

Frogspawn
A newly-laid egg looks like a black dot in clear jelly.

7–12 weeks
The tadpole grows back and front legs.

2 years
Adult frogs go to a pond to find a mate and lay eggs.

15 weeks
The tadpole becomes a froglet. It leaves the pond.

Glossary

algae tiny water plants with no leaves, stems or roots

croak to make a deep harsh sound

fertilise to make a female's eggs ready to grow by spreading **sperm** over them

gills part of a fish or tadpole used to breathe underwater

hatch to come out of an egg

lungs part of the body that animals use to breathe air

mate the male or female partner of an animal

oxygen a gas in the air and in water that living things breathe

prey the creatures that an animal hunts and eats

shallow not deep

sperm this mixes with a female's eggs to make new babies

webbed feet feet with skin stretched between the toes

Index